W9-AAA-186

A LETTER FROM PETER MUNK

Since we started the Munk Debates, my wife, Melanie, and I have been deeply gratified at how quickly they have captured the public's imagination. From the time of our first event in May 2008, we have hosted what I believe are some of the most exciting public policy debates in Canada and internationally. Global in focus, the Munk Debates have tackled a range of issues, such as humanitarian intervention, the effectiveness of foreign aid, the threat of global warming, religion's impact on geopolitics, the rise of China, and the decline of Europe. These compelling topics have served as intellectual and ethical grist for some of the world's most important thinkers and doers, from Henry Kissinger to Tony Blair, Christopher Hitchens to Paul Krugman, Peter Mandelson to Fareed Zakaria.

The issues raised at the Munk Debates have not only fostered public awareness, but they have also helped many of us become more involved and, therefore, less intimidated by the concept of globalization. It is so easy to be inward-looking. It is so easy to be xenophobic. It is so easy to be nationalistic. It is hard to go into the unknown. Globalization, for many people, is an abstract concept at best. The purpose of this debate series is to help people feel more familiar with our fast-changing world and more comfortable participating in the universal dialogue about the issues and events that will shape our collective future.

I don't need to tell you that that there are many, many burning issues. Global warming, the plight of extreme poverty, genocide, our shaky financial order: these are just a few of the critical issues that matter to people. And it seems to me, and to my foundation board members, that the quality of the public dialogue on these critical issues diminishes in direct proportion to the salience and number of these issues clamouring for our attention. By trying to highlight the most important issues at crucial moments in the global conversation, these debates not only profile the ideas and opinions of some of the world's brightest thinkers, but they also crystallize public passion and knowledge, helping to tackle some of the challenges confronting humankind.

I have learned in life — and I'm sure many of you will share this view — that challenges bring out the best in us. I hope you'll agree that the participants in these debates challenge not only each other but also each of us to think clearly and logically about important problems facing our world.

Peter Munk
Founder, Aurea Foundation
Toronto, Ontario

IS THIS THE END
OF THE LIBERAL
INTERNATIONAL
ORDER?

NIALL FERGUSON VS. FAREED ZAKARIA

THE MUNK DEBATE
ON GEOPOLITICS

Edited by Rudyard Griffiths

ANANSI

Copyright © 2017 Aurea Foundation
"Niall Ferguson and Fareed Zakaria in Conversation"
by Rudyard Griffiths. Copyright © 2017 Aurea Foundation.

All rights reserved. No part of this publication may be reproduced or
transmitted in any form or by any means, electronic or mechanical, including
photocopying, recording, or any information storage and retrieval system,
without permission in writing from the publisher.

This edition published in 2017 by
House of Anansi Press Inc.
www.houseofanansi.com

House of Anansi Press is committed to protecting our natural environment. As
part of our efforts, the interior of this book is printed on paper that contains
100% post-consumer recycled fibres, is acid-free, and is processed chlorine-free.

21 20 19 18 17   2 3 4 5

Library and Archives Canada Cataloguing in Publication

Is This the End of the Liberal International Order? : The Munk Debate
On Geopolitics / edited by Rudyard Griffiths.

(The Munk debates)
Issued in print and electronic formats.
ISBN 978-1-4870-0335-7 (softcover).—ISBN 978-1-4870-0336-4
(EPUB).—ISBN 978-1-4870-0337-1 (Kindle)

1. Geopolitics—Forecasting. I. Ferguson, Niall, panelist
II. Zakaria, Fareed, panelist III. Griffiths, Rudyard, editor
IV. Series: Munk debates

JC319.F88 2017   320.1'2   C2017-903520-7
                           C2017-903521-5

Library of Congress Control Number: 2017945105

Cover design: Alysia Shewchuk
Typesetting: Sara Loos
Transcription: Transcript Heroes

 Canada Council
for the Arts

Conseil des Arts
du Canada

 ONTARIO ARTS COUNCIL
CONSEIL DES ARTS DE L'ONTARIO
an Ontario government agency
un organisme du gouvernement de l'Ontario

*We acknowledge for their financial support of our publishing program the Canada
Council for the Arts, the Ontario Arts Council, and the Government of Canada through
the Canada Book Fund.*

CONTENTS

Is This the End of the Liberal International Order?

Pro: Niall Ferguson
Con: Fareed Zakaria

April 28, 2017
Toronto, Ontario

RUDYARD GRIFFITHS: My name is Rudyard Griffiths, and it's my privilege to once again serve as your moderator. I want to start tonight's proceedings by welcoming the North America–wide television audience tuning in to this debate right now on C-SPAN, across the continental United States, and on CPAC, from coast to coast to coast in Canada.

A warm hello also to our online audience watching this debate live, right now, on Facebook Live, our exclusive social media partner, and on Bloomberg.com, courtesy of Bloomberg Media. It's great to have you as virtual participants in tonight's proceedings. And hello to you, the over three thousand people who have filled Roy Thomson Hall to capacity for yet another Munk Debate. This is just great to see again.

This evening marks a milestone in this debate series. This is our twentieth semi-annual contest, and our ability, debate after debate, to bring you what we think are some of the brightest minds, the sharpest thinkers on the big global issues of our time, would not be possible without the generosity and the public-spiritedness of our hosts tonight. Ladies and gentlemen, an appreciation of Peter and Melanie Munk and the Aurea Foundation. Thank you both. Well done.

As I mentioned, this is a special occasion for us, our twentieth debate. So, for only the second time in the history of this series, we're convening a one-on-one contest. Our topic is the key geopolitical question of the moment: Can the process of globalization, both economic and political, that has defined the international system since the end of World War II, survive an era of rising nationalism, protectionism, and populism?

To find out, let's get our two debaters out here, centre stage, to square off on the resolution, "Be it resolved: the liberal international order is over." Ladies and gentlemen, please welcome your debater arguing for tonight's motion — the renowned historian, filmmaker, and best-selling author, Niall Ferguson.

Niall's opponent tonight, arguing against the motion, "Be it resolved: the liberal international order is over," is CNN anchor, celebrated author, and big geopolitical thinker Fareed Zakaria.

Gentlemen, thank you for being here. This is going to be an exciting debate, and I just want to run through a few, quick, pre-debate items with you. First, for those of you watching online, those of you in the audience, and Fareed and Niall, if you wish, there is a hashtag

— #Munkdebate — so you can all be part of the conversation. Also, we've got a rolling poll going. You can analyze, comment, and judge our debaters' performance throughout the debate at www.munkdebates.com/vote. And we've also got our trusty countdown clock, a key piece of the success of these debates. This clock is going to count down to zero for each of the different segments of the debate. And when you see it count down, join me in a round of applause. That will keep our debate on time and our debaters on their toes.

Now, a fun and critical data point. At the top of the evening, all of you here, the thousand people in attendance, voted on tonight's resolution as you were coming into this hall. "Be it resolved: the liberal international order is over," yay or nay. Let's see those results. The pre-audience vote: 34 percent agree, 66 percent disagree. Interesting. The room is in play.

Now, this is a critical question that we ask just to get a sense of the variability tonight: Depending on what you hear during the debate, are you open to changing your vote? Let's have those numbers, please: 93 percent. So, wow — 93 percent are open to changing. This debate is in motion, it's fluid.

Let's get it started with our opening statements. Niall Ferguson, since you're speaking in favour of the resolution, you'll go first. You've got ten minutes on the clock.

NIALL FERGUSON: Well, thank you very much indeed, Rudyard. And thank you, Peter and Melanie, for giving us the opportunity to discuss this extraordinarily important issue.

Voltaire famously said that the Holy Roman Empire was neither holy nor Roman, nor an empire. And I think the same can be said of the liberal international order. It's neither liberal nor international nor, for that matter, very orderly. And yet it seems reckless at best to come to, of all places, Toronto, and try to get people to vote against those three words, because you're all liberal. And you're all international and, by my own experience, at least, you're all quite orderly. But it seems to be that one way of thinking about this is: How difficult would it be to get you to vote in favour of what I suppose would be the opposite, which would be "conservative home-grown chaos"?

Now, we're trying that in the United States at the moment, and I just want to make it very clear that I am not here to defend Donald Trump. I'm not even here to persuade you that the liberal international order is necessarily all bad. I'm just here to persuade you that it's over.

I think there should be some full disclosure, Fareed. You and I have been amongst the beneficiaries of the liberal international order. Not quite as much as Peter, but some. We've had our fun at Davos and Aspen over the years — I think you still go to those places. And I'm not going to deny that it's been pretty good. The question I want to address is whether or not it's been good for a whole lot of other people who may not be so well represented in this audience tonight.

Has it been good for ordinary Americans? North Americans, Canadians, and U.S. citizens? Has it been good for ordinary Europeans? Has it been good for the people in the places we come from? Those Glaswegians who didn't make it to Toronto. Quite a lot tried. Or the Indian Muslims who didn't make it onto CNN. That really seems to me the point.

And I want to suggest to you tonight that we need to consider very seriously the possibility that globalization has overshot. And that in overshooting, it caused at least two major crises, the consequences of which we're still living with: the financial crisis, and then a crisis of mass migration. And if we carry on telling ourselves this story — and the story goes something like this: "Oh, we've been so much more peaceful and prosperous since 1945, thanks to those nice, liberal, international institutions, the United Nations (UN), the International Monetary Fund (IMF), the World Trade Organization (WTO), and so on. Ah! Why must these beastly populists spoil it all?" — that seems to me to be an extremely dangerous narrative for us to cling to. I don't think it's even good history to explain peace and prosperity in that way. In fact, I think it may be "fake history." Let me explain why I think that.

Why is it not liberal? Because the principal beneficiary of this wonderful liberal international order has been China. Yes. China has been the principal winner. Back in 1980, China accounted for perhaps 2 percent of the world economy. And the U.S. and Canada together were about a quarter of the world economy.

What are the percentages now? Today, China accounts for 18 percent of the world economy, and the U.S. and Canada together slightly less, 17 percent. And on present trends, that differential will grow. By 2021, the IMF says, China will account for a fifth of the world economy.

How can it be a liberal international order if the principal beneficiary is a one-party state run by a communist elite?

And they're not the only beneficiaries. Fareed, you wrote a terrific article back in 1997 about illiberal democracies. Well, the illiberal democracies, the ones with elections but no rule of law, also turn out to have done rather well from this system. I looked at some of the measures you used in that article. I wanted to see if the world had got any more free since you wrote that article. It hasn't. The proportion of countries that count as free is about the same as it was in 1997. And some of the world's countries are getting less free by the day. Dramatic declines in freedom have happened not only in Russia but in countries like Venezuela. China, the principal beneficiary of the liberal international order, ranks 173rd out of 195 in terms of freedom today. Some liberal order.

Some international order, too. Let's ask ourselves who really has benefited from this era of globalization. It's really an inter-elitist order that we should be talking about, because the principal beneficiaries of the system turn out to be those lucky few who possess rare intellectual property, or rare, real assets, including — and Peter knows this as well as anybody — commodities.

Even Canada has experienced rising inequality in this era of liberal international order. Your Gini coefficient has gone up since the 1980s. A third of the gains that this economy made in the glorious decade before the financial crisis accrued to the top one percent of income earners. The share of income in Canada that goes to the top 0.1 percent today is as high as it was before World War II.

That's another consequence of the liberal international order.

The winners take all in this system. It's one of the paradoxes of globalization. And if I'm right about that, it's signified by the fact that it's not only populists who are trying to rein in globalization. Here in Canada, you've just imposed an additional stamp tax on foreign investors in housing because of the dramatic increase in the cost of housing that has occurred as Chinese and other investors have poured into the Vancouver and Toronto markets. Toronto housing prices have gone up by a factor of three since the year 2000.

Let me conclude by observing that the liberal international order isn't orderly. The order in any case wasn't produced by the UN, much less by the World Trade Organization. It was produced by the United States and the military and other alliances that it led — a point that Fareed himself has made often in print. Let's not confuse these things. It's very different if the world is led by a Pax Americana based on American power as opposed to collective security based on the UN.

As the challenge has been made to that Pax Americana, what have we seen? Increased disorder. Islamic extremism, claiming tens of thousands of lives every year. Tens of millions of people displaced from their homes. Nuclear proliferation — the Koreans fired another missile tonight. Luckily, it didn't work. This, we're calling order? That seems to me a misnomer.

Ladies and gentlemen, we don't need to support Donald Trump to know that there's something wrong here. You don't need to be a populist. You can do it as a classical liberal, which is what I consider myself, and recognize that the biggest threat to classical liberalism is an unfettered globalization that undermines the foundations of a free society based on the rule of law and representative government.

So, the liberal international order, spelled L-I-O, ladies and gentlemen, is an L-I-E. It is neither liberal nor truly international, and it certainly isn't orderly. Folks, it's over.

Thank you very much.

RUDYARD GRIFFITHS: Powerful opening statement. And now we'll call on Fareed Zakaria. Your ten minutes are on the clock.

FAREED ZAKARIA: Thank you, Rudyard. It's a great pleasure to be here. I have to confess, I was nervous when I was told I would be going up against Niall Ferguson. You know, I do not have his erudition, I do not have his Oxford degrees, and I certainly don't have the British accent. And I thought — you know — he would have these extraordinary moments of eloquence. He began by quoting Voltaire. I'm a simple guy; I can't do all that. I'm just going to tell you a story.

I'm going to tell you a story of how this liberal international order began. And it's an interesting story because it involves a Canadian. About a year after Pearl Harbor, Franklin Roosevelt decided to try to figure out what kind of world the United States wanted to build at the end of

World War II. He could already see, believe it or not, that the United States would decisively win the war.

And he didn't have anybody he could talk to that he really trusted except Canadian prime minister Mackenzie King, who was a confidante of his. Roosevelt asked King to come to Washington. And King took the train from Ottawa down to Washington, and they sat down at dinner. Roosevelt had a martini — he didn't offer Mackenzie King a drink because he knew he was a teetotaller — and then they went to the Oval Office. And Franklin Roosevelt, this ageing visionary man, described to him what kind of world he wanted to build.

Mackenzie King kept a diary, and so it is one of the rare instances where we have Roosevelt's vision recorded. And it basically was an understanding that the world had so far been characterized by war, great-power conflict, colonial empires, economic mercantilism, and exploitation. And Roosevelt said, The United States cannot support the resurrection of that old order. We are going to try and do something different. We are going to try and build a new international order.

He didn't quite call it a liberal international order, but that was clearly what he meant. And it is a world in which, he said, first we will ask for the absolute surrender, the unconditional surrender, of the Axis powers. We will also ask the British and French to understand that they cannot reconstruct their great empires, that we need a world in which freedom and liberty and self-determination have a much greater scope.

He wanted a world of open trade and open economics. He wanted a world of greater commerce and contact. But he also wanted a world that had more rules, and so some political structures would be built that allowed for a somewhat more orderly resolution of political disputes. And that, he called the United Nations.

All these things together, in Roosevelt's view, would justify the great American effort and involvement in World War II. Now, at the end of World War II, Roosevelt did not live to build that vision, but he talked about it throughout the war and he worked on it throughout the war. And in fact, what happened was a partial creation of exactly that vision.

After hundreds and hundreds of years of something completely different, perhaps thousands of years of something different, there *was* built this liberal international order. There *was* created a rule-based system. There *was* created an open economy with greater commerce and contact.

It wasn't perfect. There were many, many flaws. And there were lots of countries that were not part of it, the Soviet Union and its allies being the most important exceptions. But it did create a new world, and if you think about the world we live in, it is the world that Franklin Roosevelt created and dreamed of with Mackenzie King.

It is a world of much greater order, much less political violence, much greater trade, commerce, contact, and capitalism, and much greater broad, sustained prosperity than has ever been true before. That's the world we live in — and that we take for granted because it has now become so commonplace. And it becomes easy to attack the little flaws, the challenges, the pauses that take place, the tiny reversions that take place when you have a world like that.

So, just look at the big picture. Steven Pinker, a Harvard professor who was a colleague of Niall's, wrote a book in which he meticulously calculated that we are now living in the most peaceful age in human history. Violence, political violence, war, civil war, and yes, terrorism, is down 75 percent compared with four or five decades ago. And it's probably down 90 or 95 percent from five hundred years ago, or at least so he claims. I'm not sure.

The data from the late Middle Ages is not very good, so I'm not sure one can speak with confidence about that, but he's a Harvard professor so I trust him. I think that when you look at the expansion of this world, you see the ineluctable power, the endurance, and the appeal of it. It started, as I said, without the great Soviet empire; it started without most of the Third World. But then, by the '50s and '60s, countries began to realize that in order to grow fast you needed to be part of it.

And so, Japan and Taiwan and South Korea start to come in, and then Latin American countries start to join. And then, of course, you have the collapse of the Soviet Union, the collapse of communism, and, all of a sudden, the entire world becomes part of this system. So, the free-trading system, the so-called General Agreement on Tariffs and Trade, or GATT, had seventy countries, seventy-eight countries in 1970. It now has 170. If you look at the European Union (EU), which had six countries in 1970, it now has twenty-eight — twenty-seven when they kick out Niall's Great Britain. But still an enormous expansion from that time.

This is the way in which all these groups have grown. And they include most powerfully, of course, the new rising and emerging powers in Asia. Niall talked about who this order has empowered. Well, I will tell you who it has empowered more than anybody else. It has empowered the poorest people in the world. The United Nations calculates that in the last fifty years, we have taken more people out of poverty than in the preceding five hundred.

And that is principally because countries like India and China were able to grow and raise their living standards and allow peasants who were living on a dollar a day to move out of poverty. I know this world well because my father was a politician. His constituency was largely rural. There were a thousand villages in it. When you went to India thirty or forty years ago, and you went into those villages, people lived lives that looked as if they were from the Middle Ages.

And today when you go to those places, it is a world transformed. They have food. They have medicine. They have shelter. It's not luxury by any standard, but it is the difference between living on a dollar a day and living on three or four dollars a day. And that transformation has taken place in India and China. It has taken place in Latin America. It has taken place in other parts of Asia, and it is beginning to take place in Africa. Those are the people who have most powerfully benefited from this new liberal international order.

But others have as well. It is not as though the United States has been standing still. The U.S. gross domestic product (GDP) is up 1,000 percent since 1970. European GDP is not up quite that much, but if you go to any of these countries, you are struck by the fact that they are rich societies. There *is* a problem with inequality; there *is* a problem with how this wealth has been redistributed; and there *is* the reality that people are culturally anxious when they see as much change as there has been in the last thirty years.

We have globalized very fast, and we have had enormous amounts of immigration. And women have been emancipated. All these changes produce cultural anxiety, and they make people want to go back to a simpler time to make America great again, to make Britain great again. But you know what? These countries have been great because they led and spearheaded this liberal international order.

They have found a way to allow the world to share in this extraordinary dream that Franklin Roosevelt had, that he discussed with Mackenzie King. It is a dream that brought Peter Munk from Hungary, fleeing persecution, here to Canada. It's a dream that brought me from India to the United States to make a family and a life for myself. It is a world that allowed Niall Ferguson to leave Scotland and then Britain, and then come to the United States and fall in love with a woman who was born in Somalia and fled to Holland to find freedom there. And then to the United States. It is where they have had their son, a beautiful boy named Thomas. Tiny Thomas, Niall calls him.

I think that Thomas's future rests on an open, plural, diverse, cosmopolitan world, where people think of you based on the content of your character, not the colour of your skin.

I think that is the world that Niall secretly believes is powerful, deep, and enduring. Otherwise, he would not have voted with his feet and moved to Palo Alto in the United States because he knows that that is where they are inventing the future and he wants to be a part of it.

So, what I say to you, Niall Ferguson, is come home. Come home to the liberal international order. Come home to the liberal international order that has been so good to you and that will be so good to your son, Thomas.

RUDYARD GRIFFITHS: Wow! This is what you get when you put two just fabulous debaters on stage, like this, head to head. We're now going to move into two rounds of rebuttals. Each of you is going to have three minutes on the clock, uninterrupted, to react to what you've heard in each other's opening statements. Niall, you're up first.

NIALL FERGUSON: Now he's crossed the line, because he's brought my children into it. You should not have done that! That wasn't smart; you're going to regret it.

So, Franklin Roosevelt had a vision, but what was the reality? The reality was that the United Nations was permanently gridlocked because of the veto exerted by members of its permanent members, the Security Council.

And in practice, what the U.S. did was to dismantle other people's empires and then build one of its own — with, I think it's fair to say, mixed results. So, I don't think we should fall into the trap, as I said earlier, of believing that the relative peace of the period after 1945 had much to do with the institutions that Franklin Roosevelt discussed after that martini with Mackenzie King.

On the contrary, it's an illusion, it's fake history to credit the relative peace of the post-1945 period to those institutions. It's an incorrect inference. The reality was that there was considerable violence, and it was a lot like the violence before. Violence between two great empires — the United States and the Soviet Union — both of which pretended they weren't empires. Steven Pinker's book will be like Norman Angell's *Great Illusion*, proven wrong at the first nuclear war that happens. The potential is there to invalidate that entire thesis in a day.

Yes, people have been pulled out of poverty in China and India. But Fareed, you know as well as I do that the principal reason is that those countries abandoned — respectively — communism and state socialism, and embraced market reforms in their own domestic policies. Once again, it's an incorrect inference to say they grew because of a liberal international order. No, they grew because they realized that state control of the private sector does not work.

You mentioned Thomas. You know, it means a lot to me that we live in the United States, because we live in a society based on the rule of law, on representative government, on a constitution that has withstood all the challenges it faced and will withstand the current challenges of populism and demagogy. That's why we chose it, because my wife can be safe in that country, safer than she ever was in Western Europe. It's not got to do with the kind of "glo-baloney" that, frankly, you're talking tonight.

FAREED ZAKARIA: I thought what I'd do is talk about China, because clearly that is the elephant in the room, as it were — the country that Niall rightly says has benefited the most from this liberal international order. It is not simply that it has grown fast because it has embraced capitalism, though capitalism is a core part of the liberal international order.

The word "liberal," of course, is "of or pertaining to liberty." The first time that phrase was used was by a Scottish Enlightenment thinker, a forerunner of Niall Ferguson, in a sense, William Robertson. The second man to use it was Adam Smith. Both used it in the specific context of capitalism and free trade. But China's embrace has not just been that. It has been a broader embrace of order.

If you think of Mao's China, this was a country that threatened routinely to have nuclear war blow up the world. And Mao said, At least that way there will be a few communists left and all the capitalists would be dead. China has moved from that place to a remarkably more rule-based acceptance of the liberal international order. It wanted desperately to become part of the World Trade Organization. It is now desperately seeking greater and greater influence at the United Nations.

China is now the second-largest supporter of peace-keeping operations around the world. It wants to become the second-largest funder of the United Nations in general. It has become far more involved in nuclear security issues, supporting the Comprehensive Nuclear-Test-Ban Treaty, supporting the Nuclear Non-Proliferation Treaty. Remember, these are all things that Mao's China believed were terrible, vicious, American imperialist plots to keep the world down.

Now, the Chinese actively want to be part of that. They want to try to solve the problems that arise. If you look at how they're handling North Korea, again they are moving to a more constructive, co-operative approach, where they're involving regional actors. They want to resurrect some kind of regional diplomacy.

This is not perfect; of course it's not.

Of course power still matters. Of course the old *realpolitik* rules still live. But what Roosevelt was trying to do was put in place some degree of regularity, some kind of norms, some kind of procedures that might help tame some of these savage winds of war. And I think if you look at the challenges we face — the extraordinary effort to incorporate the rest of the world into this system, the rise of nuclear weapons, the dangers that that poses, the dangers of chemical and biological weapons and their spread — and look at how we have managed to deal with some of these issues — for example, the outbreak of Ebola, the outbreak of other kinds of diseases — these successes have occurred through international co-operation, through greater and greater consultation.

Of course, some of it has involved the UN, some of it has not. But surely that is the kind of world we want, rather than one where we hope somehow that the countries that have nuclear weapons won't use them, or where the United States could just keep threatening to blow countries off the face of the earth. So, the liberal international order is inevitable because the alternative is unthinkable.

RUDYARD GRIFFITHS: Niall, you're up with your second rebuttal.

NIALL FERGUSON: I want to talk about history now. You see, what troubles me most about Fareed's argument is that we have heard something very similar before. If you go back to the late nineteenth century, there were a great many people who believed that a new, international order could be based on what we now call globalization. The idea of an international liberal order was there before World War I, at a time when the forces that we've seen in our time were extraordinarily, powerfully, at work.

In the period of the late nineteenth century, international migration reached levels that we have now begun to see again in our time. The percentage of the U.S. population that was foreign-born reached about 14 percent in the 1880s. Free trade reached new heights. International exchange of goods, international capital flows — all of these things reached unprecedented levels.

And liberal intellectuals — and don't be bashful, Fareed; I know you went to Yale and have a PhD from Harvard — liberal intellectuals then made the exact same mistake that Fareed Zakaria and my friend Steve Pinker are making now, and that's the "everything is awesome" mistake. You know, everything is awesome if you are in a liberal bubble, as were, for example, your counterparts in the early 1900s.

Globalization brought, as John Maynard Keynes famously said, everything that he could possibly order to his room in a matter of days. Telegraphs, steamships, international trade — Norman Angell's book *The Great Illusion* said, What could possibly go wrong? There would never be something absurd as a war, given this liberal international order we've created.

And they were wrong. They were wrong because they underestimated the backlash that is generated if you allow globalization to run too far. They also overestimated the ability of international institutions to avert conflict. Who now remembers the Hague Peace Conference? So there's a warning from history here. The real history we should learn is the history of what went wrong when globalization last self-destructed.

What worries me when I hear these fairy stories about Franklin Roosevelt, the United Nations, and Tiny Thomas living happily ever after is that it is glo-baloney. And worse than that, Fareed, it's fake history. And I suspect that in your heart, you know that. Thank you.

FAREED ZAKARIA: For someone who doesn't want to be associated with Donald Trump, you've certainly used the word "fake" several times, Niall. And I have refrained from associating you with Donald Trump because I don't know how you feel about him, one way or the other. But let me just talk about the challenges that you've raised, because they're real. There's no question. Donald Trump thinks he's a singular, unique phenomenon. And in some ways, I suppose he is — his flexibility with the facts and matters like that.

But in many ways, he's part of a trend. There is this right-wing populism that is against the liberal international order, and you see it everywhere. What's striking about it is where you don't see it, though. You don't see it in Latin America much. In Latin America, they're all busily trying to integrate into the liberal international order. From Mexico to Brazil to Argentina, populism is on the decline. If you look in Asia, whether it's India, Indonesia, or Japan, you see the same thing — reformist prime ministers and presidents who are trying to integrate into the order.

Where you do see populism is in Europe and the United States. And you see it in countries in Europe that are doing very well economically, so it can't just be about economics, because Germany's powering ahead.

It can't even just be about inequality. Northern Europe has not had much of a rise of inequality, for example. The Dutch have not had a rise in their Gini coefficient — the way you measure inequality — in about twenty years. Sweden is growing very robustly. But what all these places do have are immigrants. And that has caused enormous amounts of cultural anxiety. And let's be clear: that's true, and there are some legitimate concerns. And by the way, there have been periods in the past when immigration has been restricted, even in the United States. The liberal international order still continued to grow.

What it tells you, though, is that these things can be managed. You can find ways to address inequality. You can find ways to deal with immigration. And in fact, we are in the one Western country that is *not* going through a great rise of right-wing populism — Canada — and, I would argue, it is in large measure because Canada has managed immigration quite well.

This is not something endemic to Canada; it's not in your DNA. Canada had a whites-only immigration system that had its own problems, and then it changed under Pierre Trudeau, and then Mulroney. There was an enlightened reform of it, an emphasis on a certain kind of multiculturalism and assimilation. And now you are in this extraordinary position where you watch the rise of this illiberal anti-globalist populism, but you are not feeding it. There is almost none of it in Canada today.

And so, I look at that and it gives me great hope because it tells me that there are policy solutions to the very real challenges that Niall Ferguson has brought up, and it reminds me once again that we should all, around the world, be a little bit more Canadian.

RUDYARD GRIFFITHS: Great opening to the debate. We're now going to move into the moderated portion of this, which I'm going to do very lightly. I want to start, gentlemen, by refocusing this debate a little bit, because let's remember, the resolution is, "Be it resolved: the liberal international order is over."

I think it's a secondary concern whether it's good or bad. People may choose to vote on that prerequisite, but many people in this room are trying to figure out, is it over or not? So Niall, I want to pressure-test you a bit.

Give us some examples, some concrete examples of why you think not that it's bad but that it's over, that its time has come.

NIALL FERGUSON: Well, Fareed has just said some extraordinarily optimistic things about Europe, but I would say that the European Union's current crisis is a perfect illustration of why the liberal international order is over. Remember, it's precisely one of these institutions that Fareed has held up as an example of what can work. But the truth is, it isn't working, and that's one reason why a majority of British voters opted to leave the EU.

I was very ambivalent about Brexit last year, but I came to realize why so many people in Britain voted in favour of it. They voted that way because they discerned that in two fundamental respects the European Union had become dysfunctional. It wholly mismanaged the financial crisis, massively amplifying the negative impacts on the other member states of the European Monetary Union. Britain felt very relieved not to be a part of that.

And then it massively mismanaged the migration crisis caused by a crisis in North Africa and the Middle East, which the European Union had a hand in causing, although European politicians like to pretend the migration crisis is a sort of natural disaster. But at every level, the most basic roles that we expect a state to perform, from economic management to the defence of borders, were flunked comprehensively by the European Union over the last ten years, and the British response was: we need to take back control.

That's a really important idea here, because control by sovereign states is vital if they are to retain legitimacy. What's scary in Europe is to see populists gaining strength from the failure of Fareed's beloved international institutions. And that's the argument I'm trying to make tonight.

If you're complacent — as Fareed, I'm afraid to say, has become — in your elite bubble on the Upper West Side of Manhattan, imagining that everything is awesome, and then going to Sweden to another bubble there, and then presumably to a bubble in London, you don't realize how disaffected ordinary people are in the provinces — in peripheral France, in the provincial parts of central and eastern Europe that have swung sharply away from your liberal international order.

That's the trouble. The populism that Fareed alludes to is not something I'm here to legitimize or defend. My point is precisely that it's a symptom of what is malfunctioning in this liberal international order. And I think ultimately that the European Union will fall apart because it's simply not possible to pursue a monetary policy for an entire continent and have borderless travel for an entire continent.

It's not compatible with the stability and legitimacy of the nation-states themselves. And the Brits have just been the first to realize that.

RUDYARD GRIFFITHS: Fareed, let's have you come in on that. In effect, Europe is the canary in the coal mine, and it's close to death?

FAREED ZAKARIA: I'm so glad that Niall is mingling with the people in Palo Alto, where my home would probably buy you a garage. But I think it's important to remember history here when we talk about the European Union. For the four or five hundred years before World War II, Europe was wracked by wars of the kind that almost no continent had ever seen before.

In the religious wars, for example, one-third of all Germans were killed. France and Germany went to war three times between 1850 and 1950, and dragged the world in on two of those occasions. And when you look at the European Union today, the principal achievement is that it is unthinkable that these countries, which routinely went to war for hundreds of years, will ever go to war again.

Yes, they have problems with border control; and yes, when they meet, they have debates about monetary policy; and oh, yes, it's very difficult to have monetary policy move in one direction and fiscal policy move in another. But it's a very different world from Germany invading France and Belgium — from the horrors of World War I, World War II, and all the wars before that.

So I look at the European Union, and I know it's fashionable to decry it and to talk about the bureaucracy and to talk about the sclerosis, but it is an extraordinary achievement of political and economic co-operation that should be a model for all countries in the world. That is how we want to solve problems. That is how we should.

Those great liberal internationalists of the 1900s, Normal Angell and such, did not predict, by the way, perpetual peace. Norman Angell's book did not say there would be peace forever. He said that a war within Europe would be so costly that it would make no sense, economically, to wage it. That the victor would lose economically so much by plunging the continent into chaos that it wouldn't be worth the gamble. He was proven absolutely right in that because of the interdependence that has been achieved by this order.

So, why did Britain leave? Britain has always disliked Europe. I mean, if you read John of Gaunt's speech in *Richard II*, written by Shakespeare, it's all about Britain as "this scepter'd isle," set against the scheming, disastrous, infectious, war-like, Machiavellian Europeans. This is the way Britain has always thought of itself.

It has always seen itself as a country set apart in all kinds of ways. There is the famous headline that you saw in Britain in 1900, which said "Fog Over Channel, Continent Cut Off" —

NIALL FERGUSON: That is made up, Fareed.

FAREED ZAKARIA: That is part of Britain's —

NIALL FERGUSON: That's a made-up story.

FAREED ZAKARIA: But let me just —

NIALL FERGUSON: Just to be clear, that's fake. I mean, it's a good story, but it's just not true.

FAREED ZAKARIA: Well, as we say in journalism, some stories are too good to check.

I thought that Niall might bring up the Brexit issue, and I was struck by Theresa May's declaration of independence from the European Union, in which she said, We are doing this because we want to be a global, free-trading Britain that embraces the world, that embraces greater international commerce, co-operation; that wants to remain in all the international organizations and institutions we are in. We see it as a path to global free trade and greatness.

Now, you might ask why you would then exit the largest free-trade body in the world as a process of getting to free trade. But my point is that if you look at the way in which Britain has exited the European Union as some kind of harbinger for what is happening, I would argue you're looking at the exception that proves the rule. Europe has gone from six countries to twenty-eight.

There was a lineup of countries desperately trying to get into Europe. Why? If Britain is the one country that wants to get out, why do all these other countries want to get in? Because they understand the virtue of stability, of peace, of co-operation; because they see the before-and-after picture in Europe like you have never seen anywhere in history.

NIALL FERGUSON: Can I just push back a little bit here? If you asked yourself what exactly the European Union is, calling it a free-trade area is a stretch, Fareed, because what the European Union has become — and this has been true since the Treaty of Maastricht — is an endeavour to create a quasi-federal system, what Angela Merkel calls "Bundesrepublik Europa," the Federal Republic of Europe.

In some ways, when you look closely at how Europe works — go to Brussels, and meet the people who run it, you'll see that they live very good lives. Eurocrats don't even pay tax. It's actually a wonderful product of mid-twentieth-century thinking. It's extremely bureaucratic, highly centralized. They use the world "subsidiarity," but they never actually devolve anything that they can retain control over.

It's predicated on an extraordinarily complex system of regulation, and most importantly, to my mind, those people who run it have become almost completely disconnected from the ordinary people in what I'll call provincial Europe. Now, Fareed sneers at the fact that I live near, but not in, Palo Alto — though, really Fareed, I wouldn't make jokes about real estate prices in Toronto, if I were you.

It's a reminder that Canadians themselves — that Justin Trudeau has realized that globalization has overshot. And I don't think it's wrong to draw a distinction between what the European Union has become, which is a kind of failed, centralizing, federalist state, and what Theresa May and others in London hope to achieve, because what we must wish for is a stable international order based on democratic and rule-of-law–based sovereign states.

Yes, they can certainly reach trade agreements, but those trade agreements aren't etched in stone. It's time, unquestionably, to revisit the North American Free Trade Agreement. It's far from clear that it's perfect. But that is exactly a function of what I would regard as a stable, international order: that Canada, the United States, and Mexico look at a trade agreement and establish whether it needs to be updated. That is not the situation Britain was in.

Britain was in a position where rulings made by the Council of Ministers could be imposed on the British Parliament, regardless of what the British people wished. And there's a huge difference in my mind between *that*, which seems to me the essence of Fareed's liberal international order, and the more conservative, nation-based order that historical experience shows is far more likely to produce stability.

RUDYARD GRIFFITHS: Fareed, we've got a lot of terrain to move through here, and I want to keep this debate focused on the proposition: Is it over or not? We can discuss whether it's good or bad, but ultimately the three thousand people in this room need to make up their minds on the question. Is the liberal international order at its end?

Let's come back across the Atlantic to the United States, because as Niall said in his opening remarks, some might argue that the liberal international order has had a fatal crisis of legitimacy. That by impoverishing broad sections of its own voting publics in Western democracies, it now no longer has the social consensus within the nations that it needs to further itself to advance.

How do you respond to that specific argument — that this is in fact over because of a crisis of legitimacy that it can't recover from?

FAREED ZAKARIA: Sure, let's think about that. That was much discussed after Brexit and Donald Trump, and what I would point out is that we seem to be in a slightly different moment right now. We've just had the French elections in which the person who seemed likely to win, Emmanuel Macron, a former Rothschild banker, an economic free-trader, a believer in the European Union, a believer in trans-Atlanticism, and a proud believer —

NIALL FERGUSON: Sounds like he's a good friend of yours, Fareed. You must have met him at Davos.

FAREED ZAKARIA: Exactly, exactly. The person who seems to be likely to win in Germany is Angela Merkel. But if she loses, she is likely to lose to a Social Democrat who is more pro-European than she is.

NIALL FERGUSON: You can see why we're leaving.

FAREED ZAKARIA: If you look at Donald Trump and the United States — while it is true he won the presidency, it is also true that Hillary Clinton won almost three million more votes than he did. And he now has the lowest approval ratings of any president in history, at this point in the presidency.

So, it's important for us to remember that there are many forces at play within these societies, that there are lots and lots of people who are in favour of the liberal international order, this kind of world, the world we live in, as I say. And what's most telling, and the reason I think that it's not over,

Rudyard, is because the one common factor in all of these countries is that young people are overwhelmingly in favour of the kind of world I'm describing.

It's because not only do they understand that it is inevitable — you can't stop China from growing; you can't turn technology off; you can't stop the co-operation and interdependence that comes from trade and capital flows — but they also understand that it is beneficial. They want to live in a world that is open, that is connected, that is pluralistic, that is tolerant, that is diverse.

And that is why you see these extraordinary numbers when you look at young people in the United States, when you look at young people in Europe, and even when you look at young people in Britain. Had the vote been, you know, an under-forty vote, Brexit would have lost dramatically. And that tells me something very important, which is that the future lies with this kind of world.

We are going through a period where people who are older, who have less education, who live in rural parts of the United States and Europe understandably feel anxious, and, as I say, there are policy remedies for that which we *should* employ. And they are across the board. They involve things from immigration to economics. But don't forget that the future belongs to this liberal international order.

RUDYARD GRIFFITHS: Demographics is destiny.

NIALL FERGUSON: You should always be wary of people who say that the future belongs to them, because the reality is, to answer your question, Rudyard, that peak globalization, peak liberal international order, is already in the rear-view mirror. And you can show this with some very simple measures. Trade is no longer growing at the rate that it grew prior to the financial crisis. In fact, it's significantly less important, as Fareed well knows, as a driver of global growth post-crisis.

International capital flows have been reduced, too. Notice also that the crisis of migration continues to expose the fundamental weakness of a liberal international order that can't even achieve stabilization of a common or garden civil war in a state like Syria. Right now we have sixty-five million displaced people in the world, twenty-one million who are classified by the UN as refugees.

This is not a succeeding liberal international order. It's an increasingly illiberal inter-elitist international disorder. And that is why there is so much disaffection, and that is why we see support for populists on both the left and the right. Because, remember, populism comes in two flavours. It's like ice cream in a communist country; you can have raspberry or chocolate.

Just as last year we had Bernie Sanders — who of course would've been the Democratic nominee if they hadn't rigged the Democratic nomination system — and if one looks at the French election, Fareed, I'm sorry to tell you but your pal Macron got almost no support from younger French voters. They were all behind the communist, Mélenchon. So, let's not pretend that the centre is holding when it's not.

What, in fact, we see — and this is clear from a whole range of studies that have been published recently, and if you actually do academic research, which is, it seems to me, very important if we're going to get the historical record straight — what is very striking, if one looks at all the elections all the way back to 1870, is that financial crises lead to backlashes against globalization that erode the political centre. And it's eroded from both sides, from the far left and the far right. What we see in European politics at the moment is really a rearranging of deck chairs on board the *Titanic.* And you can imagine how this will play out. Mr. Macron will doubtless win, and he will then meet Angela Merkel, or possibly Martin Schulz, and they will tell one another "everything is awesome."

And the alienation will continue. And if you haven't already read it, I do recommend Michel Houellebecq's wonderful book *Submission.* Because what Houellebecq says in *Submission* is that, yes, this election in France will go pretty much as it has gone — he got that right — but at the next election, in order to keep out the Front National candidate, Le Pen, there'll be an Islamist candidate.

And that's the critical point that we need to focus on. Not the here and now, not this week's poll, but where Europe is headed. And it's very clear to me it is on an unsustainable path. If it cannot even secure its own borders other than by making deals with yet another illiberal pseudo-democrat, Mr. Erdoğan in Turkey, if it cannot ensure even the most elementary financial stability in peripheral countries in southern Europe (remember, the Italian banks haven't gone away as a problem), all of this talk of liberal international order is just what they do at Davos and Aspen to keep their spirits up, as ever slowly and inexorably, ever smaller shrinks the deck on the *Titanic*.

RUDYARD GRIFFITHS: Fareed, I'd like to have you respond to some of the symptoms of the demise of the liberal international order that many people in this room might think about. We could look at the annexation of Crimea, the violation of another nation's sovereignty, something that was never supposed to happen after 1945.

We see, as Niall has mentioned, declining trade, but maybe more importantly, more recently, we've seen the use of chemical weapons on defenceless civilians in Syria, responded to by little more than a cosmetic military attack. Again, why are these things, in your mind, not significant events that foreshadow — or state — that the liberal international order is in decline?

FAREED ZAKARIA: Look, you can point to every bad thing that happens in the world and find a trend out of it. But the plural of anecdote is not data. And when you try to figure out what is actually happening around the world, you have to look at the aggregate data, and the aggregate data shows that political violence, by which I mean war, civil war, and terrorism, is down. It had a modest uptick last year, but over the last thirty, forty, fifty, sixty, seventy, eighty years, the chart goes way down.

NIALL FERGUSON: Hey, can I correct you, Fareed? This is a really important point, because we *are* talking about whether there's been an inflection or not. If you look at the data on armed conflict or terrorism, there was a clear upturn from 2010, which was pretty much the low point.

FAREED ZAKARIA: Yes, I agree with that.

NIALL FERGUSON: And everything that has happened since the misnamed Arab Spring has caused terrorism and armed conflict to escalate. So you can't claim that the liberal international order is in great shape. It hasn't been in great shape since 2010 at the very latest.

FAREED ZAKARIA: Let me talk about that for a second.

NIALL FERGUSON: I mean, literally twenty to thirty thousand people a year are being killed by Islamist terrorist groups like Islamic State and Boko Haram. I'm sorry, I don't find that comforting, partly because they would like to kill my wife.

FAREED ZAKARIA: Which is terrible. And thirty thousand Americans die of handgun violence every year, and that is terrible, too.

NIALL FERGUSON: But there's a difference. There *is* a difference, Fareed!

FAREED ZAKARIA: But let me, again, just broaden the scope and remind you that if you look at the world of violence right now, a striking thing happened this year. The Colombians announced a ceasefire with FARC — the

Revolutionary Armed Forces of Colombia — in an insurgency that had gone on for five decades, killed three or four hundred thousand people, displaced millions of people.

And the reason it was striking to me was that it marked the end of a kind of political violence in the Western Hemisphere. Half the world, in other words, now does not have a war, a civil war, an armed insurgency of any kind. And if you say to yourself, well, that's Latin America — well, Latin America was very violent when I came to the United States. There were armed insurgencies in five or six Latin American countries then.

The United States was funding insurgencies in places like Nicaragua. It then invaded Grenada and invaded Panama. There was a lot of stuff going on there, and that has now essentially come to an end. Violence in the world is essentially restricted to a band of places that one could call the crescent of crisis, going from Nigeria to Afghanistan. It is almost all an Islamist belt. It is worrisome.

I think Niall and I probably agree on some of the causes of it, but notice how restricted it is. You don't see it in Asia. You see it almost not in Africa, which is extraordinary. And my point here is not that bad things aren't happening in the world. There were bad things happening in the world in the 1940s, you might have noticed. There were bad things happening in the world from 1914 to 1919. There were a lot of bad things happening in the nineteenth century. But the trend that we are looking at, this broader trend, is unmistakable.

Let me make one more point, because Niall keeps talking about the European Union, and I think it's important that we understand that the people who want the European Union the most are not people who go to Davos and Aspen, but people on the ground in the poorer countries that surround Europe.

So, look at Ukraine. Why is Ukraine trying to break free of Russia's embrace — and Russia has, as a result, engaged in an act of imperialism against it? Ukraine is trying to break free because it wants to be part of this liberal international order. Now, why does it want to do that? In 1990, Ukraine and Poland faced a choice. Poland chose to be part of the European Union, part of the West, part of this liberal international order.

Ukraine, whether it chose or not, was not allowed to become part of that order. Poland and Ukraine had the same per capita GDP in 1990. Today, Ukraine's per capita GDP is one-third of Poland's. Poland is three times richer than Ukraine, having started in the same place in 1990. So when people look at that, it is those Ukrainians — ordinary Ukrainians, ordinary Poles — who understand this, and who understand, by the way, that the European Union provides them with political stability.

It provides them with all kinds of economic assistance. It provides them with the world's largest market, into which they can grow. And it provides them with some sense of order and protection. Those are the people who I look to when I ask myself, Does the European Union have a future? I couldn't care less about the bankers at Davos.

RUDYARD GRIFFITHS: I'm conscious that we've got about five minutes left in this exchange before we get to closing statements, and I want to come to you, Niall, on the point of technology. You're living not in Palo Alto, but nearby.

We are living in an age of rapid technological advancement and change, and I guess many people here might wonder, Why isn't the technological revolution that we're living through a constant bulwark to the liberal international order? Because its thrust of intention, in many ways — networks, connecting people, allowing people to talk across linguistic and national divides — would seem to supercharge liberal internationalism, not hold it back.

NIALL FERGUSON: Yeah, it's funny how that's turned out, isn't it? Not quite what Mark Zuckerberg intended when he created Facebook, that he would unwittingly create the engine that probably did more than anything else to get Donald Trump elected last year. If one looks at the impact of social networks on not only domestic but international politics, you can't really claim that it's done a great deal to help Fareed's beloved liberal international order.

And that's not entirely surprising, actually, because the unfettered growth of companies like Facebook, not to mention Google, has without question made us a more interconnected species. We really are far more interconnected than ever before. But has that promoted the values that Fareed has been pitching tonight? Actually, no, it's turned out to be a tremendously powerful engine not just for the notorious fake news but also for full-blown cyber-warfare.

Fareed ducked your question about Ukraine — rather feebly, I thought. What happened with the invasion of Ukraine was a complete failure of the liberal international order. It utterly failed to uphold not only the UN charter but also the Budapest agreements; and the annexation of Crimea by the Russian Federation is essentially now accepted by the liberal international order as "just one of those things … never mind."

Ukraine is in a state of more or less civil war. It would be wrong to call it a frozen conflict because it's really quite hot and there are periodic outbreaks of violence. The picture that Fareed paints of Latin America is also kind of baffling. Have you heard of Venezuela? Are you following events in Caracas? Populism might be on the retreat in Latin America — it is in some countries, notably Argentina — but it's putting up a ferocious rearguard action in Venezuela right now, and people are being killed in the streets of Caracas. So my sense is that we have all probably overestimated the benefits of creating a completely interconnected world.

We didn't realize that it would actually be former KGB operatives who would best understand how to unleash troll armies to try to influence democratic elections. We underestimated the extent to which an interconnected world would be a great opportunity for radical Islamists to propagate their message.

Fareed says, Oh, it's contained in a crescent of crisis. Really? Radical Islam is contained? I must say I hadn't noticed that when people were being murdered in San Bernardino, in London, in Paris. You know? Even in

Canada there have been attacks. This is a global threat, and unfortunately, the technology that we dreamt up in Silicon Valley has proved to be essentially morally neutral.

FAREED ZAKARIA: Can I just interrupt you for one thing, Niall? I think it's important to point out that the incidence of terrorism and deaths by terrorism in Europe in the 1970s was three times higher than it is today. I know it's easy to scare people because today's terrorists are Muslims and they look different and they sound different — and there are ways in which, importantly, they are dangerous — but let's not forget that Europe went through very bad stretches with terrorism. It's easy to get people all riled up about this, but the reality is that we have been through periods of violence, we have been through periods of terrorism. Yes, the Russian annexation of Crimea was a terrible thing. So was the Soviet invasion of Czechoslovakia. So was Hungary in 1956. So was the Soviet invasion of Afghanistan.

It is not as though we didn't have bad stuff happening during what you call the heyday of the liberal international order. The point is: On balance, where are things tilting? You know? If you look at Martin Luther King's great line, he said the moral arc of the universe bends slowly, but it bends toward justice.

I would argue that the arc of history bends slowly and in zigzag ways and curves, but overall it is moving toward a greater degree of freedom, because, Niall, your great hero, Margaret Thatcher, said, "When people are free to choose, they choose freedom." I believe that still, even if you don't.

RUDYARD GRIFFITHS: Okay. Well done, gentlemen. We've come up against the clock, so we're going to move now to our closing statements. These will happen in the opposite order of the opening remarks. We're going to put five minutes on the clock. Fareed, the stage is all yours.

FAREED ZAKARIA: I told you I was worried about going up against this brilliant, well-read man who reads academic papers and, as I said, has this very posh accent. But I'm going to try again to just tell you what I know. I'll tell you about a scene from my favourite movie. It's David Lean's wonderful movie, *Lawrence of Arabia*.

There's this moment where Lawrence is convincing the Arab tribes to go up against the Ottoman Empire. And to do it, he has to get them to take the Port of Aqaba, the Turkish fort. They have to go through this terrible desert. They all say, It can't be done, it's never been done before. He gets them to do it, but they leave behind an Arab soldier, a very, very important Arab soldier whom everybody loves, Gasim.

And Sharif Ali, who is played by Omar Sharif in the movie, for those of you who remember, tells Lawrence, You can't do anything about it. The desert has swallowed him up. It was his fate. It was written. Lawrence goes into the desert for a second time and manages to bring him back, and he brings him back alive and presents him to Sharif Ali, and he says to him, "Nothing is written."

And what I want to remind you is that this is active, ongoing history in the making. Nothing is written. Yes, there are all kinds of challenges to the liberal international order. There are people who are celebrating its demise, from Donald Trump to Marine Le Pen to Nigel Farage to Geert Wilders — all these people who want it to fail, who believe that they're on to something, who are exploiting the anxieties of people who perhaps don't understand the complexity of these forces, and are telling them something very simple.

Donald Trump's message, after all, to Americans, to particularly the kind of Americans Niall is talking about, is, Your life sucks, and it's because of Mexicans, Muslims, and Chinese people. The Mexicans take your jobs, the Chinese take your factories, the Muslims endanger your lives. I will beat them all up and you will be great again. It's a powerful, seductive message.

That was, by the way, the entire campaign in two minutes! But the truth is, you aren't going to get very far by beating up foreigners. You aren't going to get very far by building walls. You aren't going to get very far by closing yourself off to the world.

I feel as though I've lived through this movie. The India that I grew up in was an India that very much believed in rejecting this liberal international order because it believed it was all a Western plot, it was American imperialism, it was another version of British colonialism. And so they shielded themselves from it and said they were protecting their industries and protecting their workers and protecting their culture.

And what you got instead was corruption, decay, stagnation, and a sense of being completely isolated from the world. You lack the technological progress, you lack the dynamism, you lack the sense of hope that came from being part of this much larger world. So what I want to say to you is: Don't give in to fatalism here; don't give in to the sense that these are great forces. We can fight these forces. You can fight these forces. You don't have to give in to them. And by voting for Niall's side, you will be giving in to a certain kind of Middle Eastern fatalism. We don't believe in that. We believe that we can write our own history. We believe we make our own destiny.

And I think that as long as we remember that, and as long as we remember that in every one of these countries there are powerful forces that believe in pluralism, in diversity, in tolerance, in liberalism, in the protection of liberty — whether you're a conservative or a liberal on the political spectrum, we are all in that sense liberals — we will prevail, because honestly, there are many more of us. There are many more people like us. And there are many more people who are not scared. They are anxious, but they understand that this is the future, and they want to prepare for it.

When thinking about the prospects of the liberal international order — now more than seventy years old, weathered and worn, tried and tested — I am reminded of that great, wise poem by Alfred Lord Tennyson, "Ulysses," and its glorious closing lines: "Though much is taken, much abides; and though we are not now that strength which in old days moved earth and heaven, that which we are, we are, one equal temper of heroic hearts, made weak by time and fate, but strong in will to strive, to seek, to find, and not to yield."

Not to yield. Never yield. Never give up. I know you won't. Thank you.

RUDYARD GRIFFITHS: Niall, you get the last word.

NIALL FERGUSON: Fareed's a friend. You might not realize that, but he is. But, you know, he's also an optimist. He's a super-optimist. In some ways, Fareed was even more optimistic than me in the sense of how the United States would do, back in the day when he was a neoconservative.

If you look back through Fareed's archive — I'm a historian, so that's the kind of thing I do — you find him writing: "Cordiality between the great powers and rising global prosperity is not natural nor self-regulating. It is the product, more than anything else, of American power and purpose." Oh, that's the same guy. Just twenty years ago. September 15, 1996.

Here he was in January 2003: "American power has brought peace and liberty to countless places around the globe, especially to Western Europe. American power helped create a more civilized world in the Balkans. Despite Washington's tentative approach toward nation-building, the war in Afghanistan has vastly improved the lives of the Afghan people. And a war in Iraq — if followed by ambitious postwar reconstruction — could transform Iraq and prod reform in the Middle East."

This doesn't quite sound like the liberal international order you were talking about earlier, Fareed.

If I think about the argument that is central to much of Fareed's work, it includes a proposition about how the liberal international order will work on its principal beneficiary — as Fareed has acknowledged, China.

Here he is back in 1997: "By dealing with China," Fareed wrote, "the United States can encourage it to play by civilized international rules ... and moderate its regional ambitions. By increasingly integrating into the world economy, some ... argue, China will over time become a more liberal state."

And in his book *The Post-American World*, Fareed hadn't given up on that: "As Chinese standards of living rise, political reform is becoming an increasingly urgent issue." That's true, an increasingly urgent issue that they want to prevent from ever happening.

Fareed has also given you an optimistic view of the threat of Islamic extremism. He's always been an optimist on this score. In *The Post-American World*, he wrote: "Over the last six years, support for Bin Laden and his goals has fallen steadily throughout the Muslim world. Much more must happen to modernize the Muslim world, but the modernizers are no longer scared. The Muslim world," he wrote, "is also modernizing, though more slowly than the rest."

The "arc of history" is one of those phrases that I'm allergic to, because there is no arc in history. What there sometimes is, is a cliff. And what worries me about

Fareed's optimism is that it's the kind of optimism that leads you to walk off a cliff.

Telling yourself that the liberal international order will somehow keep you up, it's that Wile E. Coyote moment that older members of the audience will remember, when Wile E. Coyote runs off the edge of the cliff and keeps running, and for an agonizing few seconds, he thinks he's still on solid ground. But then he looks down, and he falls. History is much more like that then any kind of arc.

We don't know when the next cliff is going to come along. If one thinks back to the last great age of globalization before World War I, the most striking thing is how hard they kept running, even after they'd gone off the end of the cliff. The socialists were still planning a meeting of the International in the summer of 1914.

The statesmen kept writing their letters and their telegrams, even after the armies had been mobilized. The liberal international order is over because it has run over one of those cliffs, and like Wile E. Coyote, optimistic Fareed and his liberal international order are going to fall. Please don't go over the cliff with them.

RUDYARD GRIFFITHS: Gentlemen, a terrific debate tonight, and a sign of a great debate is that you largely made your moderator superfluous, and for that, I thank you. I also thank the Aurea Foundation, and Peter and Melanie Munk, for making these debates possible. All of you in this room have a ballot. This is your opportunity to vote again on tonight's resolution.

Let's just review where we were at the start of this evening. Of the three thousand people in this hall, 66 percent of you disagreed with the motion; 34 percent were in favour. And then we asked what percentage of you could change your mind, and which of you were open possibly to changing your vote, and look at that: only 7 percent were dug in at the beginning of the debate. So, let's see how this plays out. We're going to be taking those votes from you as you leave the hall, and for those of you watching online, we'll have the results on social media shortly. Thanks again everybody for a terrific debate. We're going to do this all again come the autumn.

Summary: The pre-debate vote was 34 percent in favour of the resolution, 66 percent against it. The final vote showed 29 percent in favour of the motion and 71 percent against. Given that more of the voters shifted to the debater against the resolution, the victory goes to Fareed Zakaria.

Pre-Debate Interviews with Rudyard Griffiths

NIALL FERGUSON IN CONVERSATION WITH
RUDYARD GRIFFITHS

RUDYARD GRIFFITHS: Ladies and gentlemen, welcome. We're here for our pre-debate interviews with our two presenters tonight. It's my pleasure to bring into this conversation Niall Ferguson, a renowned historian, filmmaker, and commentator.

Niall, it's great to have you in Toronto for this debate. This is only the second time in this series that we're going to have a one-on-one match-up: you versus Fareed Zakaria. I want to start with some first principles: define liberal international order, because there are various ways to look at that phrase and what it means. Please unpack it for us.

NIALL FERGUSON: Well, it sounds like motherhood and apple pie when you first hear those words, because who's against liberalism? And who's against international things? And order is a desirable thing too. But when you put them together, you have a potted theory of history that says, Well, the reason that the world is so awesome is that we had a liberal international order after 1945 — a whole bunch of international institutions, including the United Nations, the European Union, and the World Trade Organization — and it created this lovely global economy in which there was free movement of goods and of people and of capital, and the world has been much more peaceful and prosperous ever since. And I'm going to argue tonight that that is nonsense and is in fact fake history, which is even worse than fake news.

RUDYARD GRIFFITHS: Let's talk a bit about your critique of the liberal international order, because in addition to seeing a series of external threats, you have a conviction that part of the crisis of the liberal international order is self-inflicted. It's internal; it has to do with the electorates and what's happened to them within the Western democracies of the world.

NIALL FERGUSON: I think if one looks at what globalization has done — and let's assume that "liberal international order" is just another way of talking about globalization — it's been enormously beneficial to people like me and Fareed Zakaria, and you too, Rudyard. I mean, it's been terrific for the one percent of people who have benefited from the global integration of markets for goods and markets for capital and from migration. I'm an immigrant and so is Fareed, so it's not really surprising that we think that the liberal international order is awesome, because it's been awesome for us. The problem is, and we've seen this in the past, if you go too far in allowing the flow of goods and people and capital across borders, not everybody benefits. In fact, a substantial chunk of the population in developed countries has not benefited at all from what I'll call hyperglobalization.

The experiment was going pretty well in the '80s and '90s, but we overshot, and this overshooting in terms of immigration, capital flows, and trade has produced negative results for a lot of people at the lower end of the income distribution. Remember, most of the benefits of this liberal international order went to the top 20 percent of the income distribution in Canada, in the United States, in most European countries — and a really big chunk of that went to the top one percent. If you were at the lower end of the income distribution, didn't go to college, and were relatively unskilled, the last twenty years have been rather poor for you. In fact, you're probably worse off than you were back in 1999. And if you're trying to explain why populists have begun to attack the liberal international order and use terms like "globalist" as an insult, I think that's because a lot of people have lost out. It's not only Donald Trump; it's a whole range of candidates for elected office around the world who have started to say, We've had too much globalization. We need to dial it back. Restrict immigration. We need to renegotiate trade agreements.

And I think the most powerful critique has been of a liberal international order for finance, because taking down all constraints on international capital flows led ultimately to a succession of financial crises, the most spectacular of which was in 2008. That really hurt a lot of people, and I think that is why the populist backlash finally came after the financial crisis. I remember being interviewed in Toronto back in 2009 by the *Globe and Mail*, and they asked me what I thought the consequences of the financial crisis would be. It had just begun at the time, and the headline they came up with, which was a quote from me, was, "There will be blood," by which I meant, there will be a political backlash. Well, it has come, and I think in that sense we can no longer confidently talk about a liberal international order. It's become disorder in the sense that democracy has been disrupted; and there are parts of the world that are anything but orderly at the moment, again as a consequence of excessive globalization.

RUDYARD GRIFFITHS: Let me try a few of the counterarguments, positions that you may confront on this stage tonight. The first would be that this order has just been too successful, not necessarily in its own right but in comparison to the next best alternative. If you look at the regimes of China and Russia, some of the traditional competitors to the liberal international order, fundamentally those are just highly unattractive ways for finance, people, and societies to organize, so why isn't the success of the liberal international order inevitable based on the next best alternative not really being that great?

NIALL FERGUSON: It's funny that you should say that, Rudyard, because as far as I can see, the principle beneficiary of the liberal international order has been the People's Republic of China and the Communist Party that runs it. I don't go to Davos anymore because I've had about enough of that, but Fareed goes there each year, and I'm sure in January when he was at Davos he heard Xi Jinping, the Chinese president, defend the liberal international order. It was fascinating to hear the arguments for free trade and free capital movement coming from a Chinese communist.

That gives you a clue as to what is wrong with the liberal international order — its principle beneficiary, certainly since the 1980s, has been a one-party state that is anything but liberal politically. China has been the main beneficiary of this order, not Canada, not the United States, and not Europe; China has been the winner, and that seems to me to make the whole idea of a liberal international order rather suspect. How can it ultimately be a liberal order if its principle beneficiary is the People's Republic of China, a one-party state?

RUDYARD GRIFFITHS: Let's talk about hard power, because as a historian that's something you've written and thought a lot about. If you look at the distribution of hard power in the world, 55 percent of global defence spending originates in one country, the United States. Why isn't that an indication that the existing order will persevere, because again, the competitors to that order, in terms of the hard power that they can project against it, are Lilliputian at best.

NIALL FERGUSON: Well, we have to be a little bit careful with our terms here, because if I'm not careful everything is going to be attributed to the liberal international order, including the U.S. defence budget. Look, if the world has been relatively more peaceful since 1945 than it was in the first half of the twentieth century, which it certainly has been, the main reason is not because the United Nations was created, much less the European Union. The main reason is that the United States decided to engage as it had not in the 1920s and 1930s, and play a leadership role. Now, if you think that the U.S. defence budget is an aspect of the liberal international order, then words have lost all their meaning, because the U.S. defence budget has been maintained at a high level mainly because of conservative politicians, not because of liberal ones. It's international in the sense that the United States imposes the Pax Americana through a system of alliances and military deployments.

And yes, it is an order, but it is an order that depends on a nation-state, the strongest nation-state, the United States. It seems to me we have to draw a distinction here if we want it to have meaning. We cannot attribute the stability or relative stability of the world in the second half of the twentieth century and the first quarter of the twenty-first century to a liberal international order if the real cause is a nation-state, the United States, that has become strong mainly because conservative politicians insisted that the defence budget be maintained at a relatively high level. There is order of a sort, but it seems to me that if one takes a step back, one of the striking features of this century has been the crumbling of the Pax Americana, its loss of legitimacy, its loss of effectiveness, most obviously in Iraq, not to mention Afghanistan. So, even the order itself seems to me to be crumbling before our very eyes. I think the Pax Americana was the big story after 1945. I think the big story since 9/11 has been its crumbling.

RUDYARD GRIFFITHS: Just one last argument to try out: the idea of closed versus open systems. Proponents of the liberal international order say part of its strength is that it is an open system, that it is based on a network and expanding that network globally, which it's done arguably quite well over the last number of decades. Its competitors and its alternatives very much look like closed systems, most notably China, an autocratic state. So, in history, are there examples of open systems losing out to closed systems? And why aren't people right to think that open systems always win?

NIALL FERGUSON: I think you're maybe going to confuse listeners if you think the distinction is between a liberal international order and China, or some other authoritarian regime, because in fact the liberal international order has been very beneficial to politically closed societies like China. And indeed, the main beneficiaries of globalization since the 1980s have been states like China that have embraced the rules of the road when it comes to trade, and to some extent also to capital movements, but have not made any concessions on the issue of democracy. This is the paradox of our time: yes, there was a liberal international order in the sense that we created institutions like the World Trade Organization and the International Monetary Fund, and we created rules for the global economy. And then we said that the Chinese, if they wanted to, could come play. And we bent those rules quite significantly so that the Chinese could join the WTO, and their currency could become part of the IMF Special Drawing Right. And they've taken full advantage of the system that was created. It hasn't made them any more liberal; in fact, it's relegitimized their system of one-party state rule without the rule of law. And that's the central weakness of this entire project.

We told ourselves — remember Bill Clinton making this argument — that if we only had a system of free trade then the authoritarians of the world would politically transition to our wonderful democratic system. This was Francis Fukuyama's vision in "The End of History?" Well, guess what? It didn't work out that way. What has actually happened is that illiberal pseudo-democracies and full-blown authoritarian regimes like China have done very well on the back of globalization. They've greatly increased their share of GDP. You know, China's share of GDP is now larger than that of the United States and Canada combined on a purchasing power parity basis. That trend is only going to continue. So, they've been the winners of this wonderful liberal international order, which makes me wonder if it's a bit like what Voltaire said of the Holy Roman Empire, that it was neither holy nor Roman nor an empire. Well, the thing about the liberal international order is that it's neither liberal nor very international nor very orderly.

RUDYARD GRIFFITHS: Interesting point. I want to end on your thoughts as to what you might look for next in terms of symptoms or signs that the liberal international order really is under acute pressure and stress, and may be heading toward some kind of end. We've talked about Brexit and Trump as symptoms of the decline of the liberal international order, but what would you look for next to herald some more significant change?

NIALL FERGUSON: The naive view is to say, "Well, the populists are going to win all elections forevermore," and then to say when they don't, "There you are, this was all over-hyped." I think the populist backlash that we saw in the English-speaking world last year is only part of the story. We saw already in 2008 a financial crisis that revealed the fragility of the international financial system. I think it's still very fragile, and I wouldn't be surprised if we saw another financial crisis in the relatively near future, quite possibly emanating from China. Then you have to ask yourself, is this wonderful system capable of delivering order to the most disorderly part of the world — North Africa and the Middle East? Well, there's not much sign of it at this point, and my fear is that things are going to get worse before they get better, not only in Syria and Iraq, but further afield where we have a problem of escalating conflict and state failure. So, if one is looking for signs of a future crisis, don't just look at politics, don't just look at populism — that's only one of the symptoms that this liberal international order is in trouble. Look instead for the next financial crisis and then look for the next conflict.

The big lesson from history, Rudyard, and this is the point I want to make tonight, is that we've run the experiment of hyperglobalization before, in the late nineteenth century. There were almost no restrictions on migration and trade, and capital flowed across borders with almost no regulation. This was a very globalized world, and at the time, the one percent who benefited from it were tremendously happy. And people wrote books, a bit like Fareed did, saying that in this wonderful new order there will never be another war because everything is awesome. Unfortunately, the populist backlash was just the beginning of a succession of crises that ultimately culminated in 1914 with World War I. War can be global too, and we'll know that the liberal international order has truly failed when it does what the last iteration did in the early twentieth century, and that is to produce a major conflict.

RUDYARD GRIFFITHS: Sobering words, Niall, and we're going to hear a lot more tonight. Thank you for coming to Toronto. You've got a debate to prepare for, so I'm going to let you go do that, but, again, great to have your input and analysis.

NIALL FERGUSON: Thanks, Rudyard.

FAREED ZAKARIA IN CONVERSATION WITH
RUDYARD GRIFFITHS

RUDYARD GRIFFITHS: Fareed Zakaria is the host of the top-rated CNN show *GPS*, a bestselling author, and a much sought-after voice on geopolitics and international affairs.

Fareed, it's great to have you here in Toronto for another Munk Debate. This is our twentieth debate in the series, and it's only the second time that we're featuring a one-on-one debate, so I'm really excited to see how this works out. I think it's going to allow the debate to breathe a bit between you and Niall. I thought it could be helpful to our audience in advance of tonight's debate to have you define the liberal international order, because there are a variety of ways to understand it historically, how it's evolved, and what it constitutes today.

FAREED ZAKARIA: Thanks, Rudyard. It's always a pleasure. The Munk Debates are frankly one of the most extraordinary intellectual events that have been created in these last few decades, and a lot of that credit goes to you.

I think of the liberal international order very simply. It's the world we live in; it's the world that we have come to take for granted but that is actually very, very unusual. If you think about it, for most of human history, the world has been characterized by constant power struggles, wars, and economic crises. Relations between countries have been largely conflictual, predatory, mercantilist — that's been the world for most of human history. And then, after World War II, the major countries of the world, led by the United States, decided to try something different. They decided to try to create a more stable world, a world that had some modicum of order, where there was openness in terms of economics, in terms of trade, where openness in politics was encouraged so that democracy became an aspirational quality, and where human rights were observed more routinely than they had been, through a series of conventions and laws and things like that.

Now, it's important to point out that this is not a perfect world. Of course there have been wars; of course there have been huge human rights violations — but what's actually striking is the degree to which the vision that people like Franklin Roosevelt, Harry Truman, and Mackenzie King had has actually borne out, so the rates of violence as measured by most people are dramatically down over the last thirty, forty, fifty, and sixty years.

Great-power competition of the kind that was normal has gone away. We've created an open world economy where trade, capital flows, and growth have gone up and up, pulling all kinds of countries out of poverty, from Latin America to China. And there has been a greater observance of human rights, particularly among the major civilized powers of the world. Now, you might say, Oh, but that was normal, that's ordinary. No, actually it was not. Germany, to put it simply, was not a country that observed human rights norms for the first half of the twentieth century; whereas, for the second half of the twentieth century, it became an exemplary country. The same is true of countries like France and Britain in their colonial empires. There's been a dramatic transformation that we've grown accustomed to. It's like the air we breathe; we don't notice it. But like air, if you took it away, we'd be living in a very different world.

RUDYARD GRIFFITHS: The stresses on that order — people point to Brexit, to the election of Trump, to the rise of populism as a resurgent political phenomenon for much of the Western world — what are these? Are these simply irritants in the liberal international order or are they graver threats to its existence?

FAREED ZAKARIA: They're all threats. Nothing works automatically. This liberal international order has its problems; it has its stresses, its strains and challenges. It's always going to be a work in progress; it's always going to require that there be fixes, adjustments, changes. I would put these challenges in two categories. The first are the internal challenges like Brexit and Trump — challenges born out of the reality that there are real stresses and strains. This is a seventy-five-year-old system; it's trying to accommodate a bunch of different new things — for one, the massive expansion of the system to include a country like China with 1.2 billion people and 400 million skilled workers. Of course that's going to have an impact. It also has to deal with new technologies — driverless cars are going to put something like three million people out of work in the United States, people who drive cars, buses, and trucks for a living. How do you handle those kinds of things? Those are really internal stresses.

An external challenge is a country like Russia, which does not really benefit as much from the international liberal order because it's an oil state. Oil states thrive on instability. The more unstable the world is, the higher the price of oil, and so those kinds of states that have a narrow, single-dimensional economy are always going to be difficult. And Putin's Russia has become a geopolitically adventurous, ambitious spoiler as well.

The first set of challenges we can fix; there are solutions to these problems. These are the richest countries in the history of the world. If you tell me that working-class people are feeling pain and are feeling a loss of status, I get it and I hear it. But I would also tell you there are solutions. There is money; there is creativity; there are ways to retrain people; there are ways to give people a future. And you can see this in a very simple statistic: young people everywhere, from the United States to Britain to Canada to France to Germany — they all want this liberal international order.

They all vote for the parties that enthusiastically embrace this liberal international order. They look forward to the idea of a pluralistic, open, diverse world. Older people who are not as able to adapt of course have their challenges. But the future, to put it bluntly, belongs to the young — not those aged sixty-five and older.

RUDYARD GRIFFITHS: So, you're in a sense saying, let's not get carried away right now in terms of the election of Trump, Le Pen in France, or the likes of Nigel Farage. This is kind of symptomatic of a peak populism that will exist for a period of time but won't necessarily undo the last seventy-five years.

FAREED ZAKARIA: That's exactly right. I think it's a real phenomenon born of real concerns and real anxieties. The part of it that is unfortunate and unsavoury is the way that most of these politicians look at the problem correctly and then blame foreigners. I don't think that in many cases foreigners are the reason for these problems; it's often technology. Beating up foreigners, expelling them, being particularly cruel to minorities — that's not going to solve the problem; that's not going to reindustrialize the Midwest in the United States. But I think that it's important to remember that these challenges will be overcome, and then there'll be new ones. I don't envision a liberal international order or an open world system where you don't have problems. Of course, you solve one set of problems and create another. That's life. What it tells you is that you have to keep working at it.

RUDYARD GRIFFITHS: Let's talk a little bit about geography. Some people would say that Europe is both the exemplar and the product of the liberal international order, a continent torn apart by war, and infected by something far worse than populism over sixty years ago. Europe today is struggling — it's struggling politically; it's struggling economically. Why shouldn't people look at Europe today and say, Maybe that's a bellwether for where the larger liberal international order is headed?

FAREED ZAKARIA: When people say this about Europe, I always say to them one very simple thing: You should go and visit Europe. When you go to Europe, when you go to France or Italy, you will discover that Europe is one of the richest parts of the world — where you can travel almost everywhere without a passport, let alone a visa, and where countries that once fought each other to the point that they decimated the entire continent, they burned down entire villages, now live so happily and amicably together that a war between France and Germany today is unthinkable, even though they fought three wars between 1850 and 1950. This is a continent where co-operation among these countries is so endemic, so enduring, that they really can't imagine any other form of life.

Now, they face a few challenges. They have an ageing demography; they have lower productivity; and they have had difficulty assimilating immigrants. But let's put it against the backdrop of this remarkable prosperity and achievement. So, yes, they're going through some struggles, and they will continue to go through them. But when you're at $50,000 per capita GDP, you don't need to grow 4 percent a year. They're expected to grow 2 percent this year, which is about what the United States will grow, but because they have fewer immigrants on a per capita basis, that's actually higher. They have less innovation in some areas, but they do very well in manufacturing. I think the picture is more mixed than people realize. They handle health care much better than the United States; they've handled pensions, for the most part, much better than the United States. In some ways, Europe looks more like Canada than the United States.

It doesn't have the oil to soften the blows, but the challenges that a place like Europe faces should not obscure the fact that the European Union remains the single most extraordinary example of political and economic co-operation in the world. Whether Britain is in or out, whether the Euro was the right idea or not — I personally think it wasn't — the idea that countries that for five hundred years tore each other apart are now living in a state of almost unity … I think we should just step back and marvel at that. At some level, isn't that the world we want? Isn't that the world that we should all aspire to? And shouldn't we be looking at that and asking, What did they get right? rather than pointing out that they've got too many retirees, or that their productivity levels are not as high as they should be. Those problems are temporary and temporal. The grand project of Europe remains one of the more inspiring ones in the world.

RUDYARD GRIFFITHS: Another part of the world I want to get your thoughts on: China. Some people would say that the liberal international order has empowered, enriched, and strengthened the world's largest autocratic state. In other words, the liberal international order has had a highly illiberal effect. What do you think of that argument?

FAREED ZAKARIA: I think one of the ironies of the liberal international order is that it does empower newcomers that are in a very different stage of historical development. If you think about the liberal international order in the nineteenth century, this was an order in a sense created, spread, and underwritten by Great Britain, and, to a certain extent, the United States as a junior partner. Who did it empower? It empowered Germany. Germany was not a particularly liberal power; it was quite a nefarious state, and it took a lot to civilize Germany. The liberal international order also empowered, in various ways, Italy and Austria-Hungary, which were also not particularly liberal powers.

Similarly, the current liberal international order has empowered China. Now, China is not nearly as illiberal or as autocratic as Germany was; in many ways, it plays by the rules and is becoming more liberal on the international scale. Look at their contribution to peacekeeping, their contribution in all kinds of intergovernmental areas, even their movement on climate change. But domestically the regime remains quite autocratic, though the people are getting more open and the economy is getting more open. One would expect and hope that over time China will become less autocratic and less illiberal. I don't think it will become a democracy any time soon, but I do think it will play by international rules more than it has. And you can already see this on a number of fronts. The Chinese are becoming more willing to get involved in intergovernmental co-operation. For example, in Iran they proved to be extremely co-operative. There are places in peacekeeping where even in Africa they are becoming much more co-operative than they were. And what's the alternative? We're talking about 1.3 billion people. You have to try to bring them in and try to find a way to make them play by the rules. Otherwise, they'll play entirely outside of the system.

So, this is a great bet that the Western world has made, that by integrating China they will civilize it in some way. I still think it's the right path. It's a bumpy path. There are going to be setbacks, and there are going to be times when it seems as though it was a bad bet, particularly economically. But remember, 400 million Chinese peasants have moved out of poverty — that's living on a dollar a day. They've moved out of that to living on four or five dollars a day. Just in terms of the measure of human achievement, that was surely worth it, outside of anything else.

RUDYARD GRIFFITHS: Finally, what would you look for in terms of signs or symptoms in the future that the liberal international order is strong, that it is enduring, and that we should be optimistic about its ability to remain the rule-setting system of the twenty-first century?

FAREED ZAKARIA: You've touched on many of them. To my mind, whether or not China remains broadly committed to this rule-based system is important. Does it want to keep participating? Right now, the Chinese keep saying, We want to be more involved in this rule-based system. We want a Chinese person to be considered for the head of the World Bank or the IMF. We want the Chinese percentage of voting to be higher in the UN. In other words, what they are asking for is not the destruction of the liberal international order but their empowerment within it as the second-largest economy in the world. The more they take responsibility, the more they participate, I think at the end of the day that is going to be better, though it will change that order a little bit to reflect the realities of a more multi-polar world.

The second indicator is this issue of young people. The degree to which young people continue to view this open world not just as inevitable but as beneficial is going to be crucial. Young people look at the same world that so many older people look at with suspicion and hostility, and they think, I am enriched economically, politically, and culturally by living in an open, diverse, pluralistic, connected world. They look at these connections; they look at the fact that they can work, live, communicate, trade, and interact with people around the world at any time as one of the core principles that animate their lives and that they want to affirm.

But young people need to understand that this doesn't happen automatically, and it won't be saved or strengthened by just pressing a "Like" button on Facebook. You have to go out there and you have to support it. You have to fight for it, you have to campaign for it, and you have to vote for it. And if you do all of that, then this world that you have come to take for granted will persist. All human endeavours, all human civilization is fragile. If you scratch, you can get some very nasty stuff coming out of the woodwork. I think that as long as young people understand that message, we'll be fine.

RUDYARD GRIFFITHS: Fareed, an important and a positive note to end on. I know you've got a debate to prepare for, so, again, great to have you here in Toronto. Thanks for coming.

FAREED ZAKARIA: Thank you, thank you.

ACKNOWLEDGEMENTS

The Munk Debates are the product of the public-spiritedness of a remarkable group of civic-minded organizations and individuals. First and foremost, these debates would not be possible without the vision and leadership of the Aurea Foundation. Founded in 2006 by Peter and Melanie Munk, the Aurea Foundation supports Canadian individuals and institutions involved in the study and development of public policy. The debates are the foundation's signature initiative, a model for the kind of substantive public policy conversation Canadians can foster globally. Since the creation of the debates in 2008, the foundation has underwritten the entire cost of each semi-annual event. The debates have also benefited from the input and advice of members of the board of the foundation, including Mark Cameron, Andrew Coyne, Devon Cross, Allan Gotlieb, Margaret MacMillan, Anthony Munk, Robert Prichard, and Janice Stein.

For her contribution to the preliminary edit of the book, the debate organizers would like to thank Jane McWhinney.

Since their inception, the Munk Debates have sought to take the discussions that happen at each event to national and international audiences. Here the debates have benefited immeasurably from a partnership with Canada's national newspaper, the *Globe and Mail*, and the counsel of its editor-in-chief, David Walmsley.

With the publication of this superb book, House of Anansi Press is helping the debates reach new audiences in Canada and around the world. The debates' organizers would like to thank Anansi chair Scott Griffin and president and publisher Sarah MacLachlan for their enthusiasm for this book project and insights into how to translate the spoken debate into a powerful written intellectual exchange.

ABOUT THE DEBATERS

NIALL FERGUSON is the Laurence A. Tisch Professor of History at Harvard University and William Ziegler Professor of Business Administration at Harvard Business School. He is also a Senior Research Fellow at Jesus College, Oxford, and a Senior Fellow at the Hoover Institution, Stanford University. He is the author of numerous bestselling books, including *The Ascent of Money*. A prolific commentator on contemporary politics and economics, Ferguson is a contributing editor for the *Financial Times* and senior columnist with *Newsweek*.

FAREED ZAKARIA is host of CNN's flagship international affairs program, *Fareed Zakaria GPS*, which won the 2012 Peabody Award. He is a contributing editor at *The Atlantic*, a *Washington Post* columnist, a former editor of *Newsweek International*, and editor-at-large of *TIME* magazine. He is the author of the international bestsellers *The Future of Freedom* and *The Post-American World: Release 2.0.* He was described by *Esquire* as "the most influential foreign policy adviser of his generation" and was included on *Foreign Policy*'s list of "Top 100 global thinkers."

ABOUT THE EDITOR

RUDYARD GRIFFITHS is the chair of the Munk Debates and president of the Aurea Charitable Foundation. In 2006 he was named one of Canada's "Top 40 under 40" by the *Globe and Mail*. He is the editor of thirteen books on history, politics, and international affairs, including *Who We Are: A Citizen's Manifesto*, which was a *Globe and Mail* Best Book of 2009 and a finalist for the Shaughnessy Cohen Prize for Political Writing. He lives in Toronto with his wife and two children.

ABOUT THE MUNK DEBATES

The Munk Debates are Canada's premier public policy event. Held semi-annually, the debates provide leading thinkers with a global forum to discuss the major public policy issues facing the world and Canada. Each event takes place in Toronto in front of a live audience, and the proceedings are covered by domestic and international media. Participants in recent Munk Debates include Anne Applebaum, Louise Arbour, Robert Bell, Tony Blair, John Bolton, Ian Bremmer, Stephen F. Cohen, Daniel Cohn-Bendit, Paul Collier, Howard Dean, Alain de Botton, Alan Dershowitz, Hernando de Soto, Maureen Dowd, Gareth Evans, Nigel Farage, Mia Farrow, Niall Ferguson, William Frist, Newt Gingrich, Malcolm Gladwell, David Gratzer, Glenn Greenwald, Stephen Harper, Michael Hayden, Rick Hillier, Christopher Hitchens, Richard Holbrooke, Josef Joffe, Robert Kagan, Garry Kasparov, Henry Kissinger, Charles Krauthammer, Paul Krugman, Arthur B. Laffer,

Lord Nigel Lawson, Stephen Lewis, David Daokui Li, Bjørn Lomborg, Lord Peter Mandelson, Elizabeth May, George Monbiot, Caitlin Moran, Dambisa Moyo, Thomas Mulcair, Vali Nasr, Alexis Ohanian, Camille Paglia, George Papandreou, Steven Pinker, Samantha Power, Vladimir Pozner, Matt Ridley, David Rosenberg, Hanna Rosin, Simon Schama, Anne-Marie Slaughter, Bret Stephens, Mark Steyn, Lawrence Summers, Justin Trudeau, Amos Yadlin, and Fareed Zakaria.

The Munk Debates are a project of the Aurea Foundation, a charitable organization established in 2006 by philanthropists Peter and Melanie Munk to promote public policy research and discussion. For more information, visit www.munkdebates.com.

ABOUT THE INTERVIEWS

Rudyard Griffiths's interviews with Niall Ferguson and Fareed Zakaria were recorded on April 28, 2017. The Aurea Foundation is gratefully acknowledged for permission to reprint excerpts from the following:

(p. 51) "Niall Ferguson in Conversation," by Rudyard Griffiths. Copyright © 2017 Aurea Foundation. Transcribed by Transcript Heroes.

(p. 61) "Fareed Zakaria in Conversation," by Rudyard Griffiths. Copyright © 2017 Aurea Foundation. Transcribed by Transcript Heroes.

The Global Refugee Crisis: How Should We Respond?
Arbour and Schama vs. Farage and Steyn

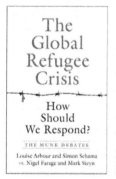

The world is facing the worst humanitarian crisis since the Second World War. Over 300,000 are dead in Syria, and one and a half million are either injured or disabled. Four and a half million people are trying to flee the country. And Syria is just one of a growing number of failed or failing states in the Middle East and North Africa. How should developed nations respond to human suffering on this mass scale? Do the prosperous societies of the West, including Canada and the United States, have a moral imperative to assist as many refugees as they reasonably and responsibly can? Or is this a time for vigilance and restraint in the face of a wave of mass migration that risks upending the tolerance and openness of the West?

"There's nothing to be ashamed of about having an emotional response to the suffering of four million Syrian refugees."
— Simon Schama

houseofanansi.com/collections/munk-debates

READ MORE FROM THE MUNK
DEBATES — CANADA'S PREMIER DEBATE SERIES

Do Humankind's Best Days Lie Ahead?
Pinker and Ridley vs. de Botton and Gladwell

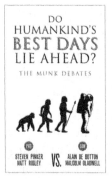

From the Enlightenment onwards, the West has had an enduring belief that through the evolution of institutions, innovations, and ideas, the human condition is improving. But is this the case? Pioneering cognitive scientist Steven Pinker and influential author Matt Ridley take on noted philosopher Alain de Botton and bestselling author Malcolm Gladwell to debate whether humankind's best days lie ahead.

"It's just a brute fact that we don't throw virgins into volcanoes any more. We don't execute people for shoplifting a cabbage. And we used to." — Steven Pinker

houseofanansi.com/collections/munk-debates

READ MORE FROM THE MUNK
DEBATES — CANADA'S PREMIER DEBATE SERIES

Should the West Engage Putin's Russia?
Cohen and Pozner vs. Applebaum and Kasparov

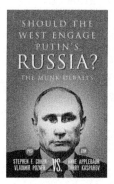 How should the West deal with Vladimir Putin? Acclaimed academic Stephen F. Cohen and veteran journalist and bestselling author Vladimir Pozner square off against internationally renowned expert on Russian history Anne Applebaum and Russian-born political dissident Garry Kasparov to debate the future of the West's relationship with Russia.

"A dictator grows into a monster when he is not confronted at an early stage ... And unlike Adolf Hitler, Vladimir Putin has nuclear weapons." — *Garry Kasparov*

houseofanansi.com/collections/munk-debates

READ MORE FROM THE MUNK
DEBATES — CANADA'S PREMIER DEBATE SERIES

Has Obama Made the World a
More Dangerous Place?
Kagan and Stephens vs. Zakaria and Slaughter

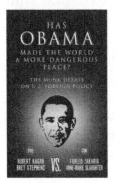

From Ukraine to the Middle East to
China, the United States is redefining
its role in international affairs. Famed
historian and foreign policy commentator Robert Kagan and Pulitzer Prize–
winning journalist Bret Stephens take
on CNN's Fareed Zakaria and noted
academic and political commentator
Anne-Marie Slaughter to debate the
foreign policy legacy of President Obama.

"Superpowers don't get to retire ... In the international sphere,
Americans have had to act as judge, jury, police, and, in the case
of military action, executioner." — Robert Kagan

houseofanansi.com/collections/munk-debates

READ MORE FROM THE MUNK
DEBATES — CANADA'S PREMIER DEBATE SERIES

Does State Spying Make Us Safer?
Hayden and Dershowitz vs. Greenwald and Ohanian

In a risk-filled world, democracies are increasingly turning to large-scale state surveillance, at home and abroad, to fight complex and unconventional threats. Former head of the CIA and NSA Michael Hayden and civil liberties lawyer Alan Dershowitz square off against journalist Glenn Greenwald and reddit co-founder Alexis Ohanian to debate if the government should be able to monitor our activities in order to keep us safe.

"Surveillance equals power. The more you know about someone, the more you can control and manipulate them in all sorts of ways." — *Glenn Greenwald*

houseofanansi.com/collections/munk-debates

READ MORE FROM THE MUNK
DEBATES — CANADA'S PREMIER DEBATE SERIES

Are Men Obsolete?
Rosin and Dowd vs. Moran and Paglia

For the first time in history, will it be better to be a woman than a man in the upcoming century? Renowned author and editor Hanna Rosin and Pulitzer Prize–winning columnist Maureen Dowd challenge *New York Times*–best-selling author Caitlin Moran and trail-blazing social critic Camille Paglia to debate the relative decline of the power and status of men in the workplace, the family, and society at large.

"Feminism was always wrong to pretend women could 'have it all.' It is not male society but Mother Nature who lays the heaviest burden on women." — *Camille Paglia*

houseofanansi.com/collections/munk-debates

Should We Tax the Rich More?
Krugman and Papandreou vs. Gingrich and Laffer

Is imposing higher taxes on the wealthy the best way for countries to reinvest in their social safety nets, education, and infrastructure while protecting the middle class? Or does raising taxes on society's wealth creators lead to capital flight, falling government revenues, and less money for the poor? Nobel Prize–winning economist Paul Krugman and former prime minister of Greece George Papandreou square off against former speaker of the U.S. House of Representatives Newt Gingrich and famed economist Arthur Laffer to debate this key issue.

"The effort to finance Big Government through higher taxes is a direct assault on civil society." — Newt Gingrich

houseofanansi.com/collections/munk-debates

READ MORE FROM THE MUNK
DEBATES — CANADA'S PREMIER DEBATE SERIES

*Can the World Tolerate an Iran
with Nuclear Weapons?*
Krauthammer and Yadlin vs. Zakaria and Nasr

Is the case for a pre-emptive strike on Iran ironclad? Or can a nuclear Iran be a stabilizing force in the Middle East? Former Israel Defense Forces head of military intelligence Amos Yadlin, Pulitzer Prize–winning political commentator Charles Krauthammer, CNN host Fareed Zakaria, and Iranian-born academic Vali Nasr debate the consequences of a nuclear-armed Iran.

"Deterring Iran is fundamentally different from deterring the Soviet Union. You could rely on the latter but not the former." — Charles Krauthammer

houseofanansi.com/collections/munk-debates

READ MORE FROM THE MUNK
DEBATES — CANADA'S PREMIER DEBATE SERIES

Has the European Experiment Failed?
Joffe and Ferguson vs. Mandelson and Cohn-Bendit

Is one of human history's most ambitious endeavours nearing collapse? Former EU commissioner for trade Peter Mandelson and EU Parliament co-president of the Greens/European Free Alliance Group Daniel Cohn-Bendit debate German publisher-editor and author Josef Joffe and renowned economic historian Niall Ferguson on the future of the European Union.

"For more than ten years, it has been the case that Europe has conducted an experiment in the impossible." — *Niall Ferguson*

houseofanansi.com/collections/munk-debates

North America's Lost Decade?
Krugman and Rosenberg vs. Summers and Bremmer

The future of the North American economy is more uncertain than ever. In this edition of the Munk Debates, Nobel Prize–winning economist Paul Krugman and chief economist and strategist at Gluskin Sheff + Associates David Rosenberg square off against former U.S. treasury secretary Lawrence Summers and bestselling author Ian Bremmer to tackle the resolution, "Be it resolved: North America faces a Japan-style era of high unemployment and slow growth."

"It's now impossible to deny the obvious, which is that we are not now, and have never been, on the road to recovery." — Paul Krugman

houseofanansi.com/collections/munk-debates

READ MORE FROM THE MUNK
DEBATES — CANADA'S PREMIER DEBATE SERIES

Does the 21st Century Belong to China?
Kissinger and Zakaria vs. Ferguson and Li

Is China's rise unstoppable? Former U.S. secretary of state Henry Kissinger and CNN's Fareed Zakaria pair off against leading historian Niall Ferguson and world-renowned Chinese economist David Daokui Li to debate China's emergence as a global force — the key geopolitical issue of our time.

This edition of the Munk Debates also features the first formal public debate Dr. Kissinger has participated in on China's future.

"I have enormous difficulty imagining a world dominated by China ... I believe the concept that any one country will dominate the world is, in itself, a misunderstanding of the world in which we live now." — Henry Kissinger

houseofanansi.com/collections/munk-debates

READ MORE FROM THE MUNK
DEBATES — CANADA'S PREMIER DEBATE SERIES

Hitchens vs. Blair

Christopher Hitchens vs. Tony Blair

Intellectual juggernaut and staunch atheist Christopher Hitchens goes head-to-head with former British prime minister Tony Blair, one of the Western world's most openly devout political leaders, on the age-old question: Is religion a force for good in the world? Few world leaders have had a greater hand in shaping current events than Blair; few writers have been more outspoken and polarizing than Hitchens.

Sharp, provocative, and thoroughly engrossing, *Hitchens vs. Blair* is a rigorous and electrifying intellectual sparring match on the contentious questions that continue to dog the topic of religion in our globalized world.

"If religious instruction were not allowed until the child had attained the age of reason, we would be living in a very different world." — Christopher Hitchens

houseofanansi.com/collections/munk-debates

READ MORE FROM THE MUNK
DEBATES — CANADA'S PREMIER DEBATE SERIES

The Munk Debates: Volume One
Edited by Rudyard Griffiths
Introduction by Peter Munk

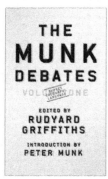

Launched in 2008 by philanthropists Peter and Melanie Munk, the Munk Debates is Canada's premier international debate series, a highly anticipated cultural event that brings together the world's brightest minds.

This volume includes the first five debates in the series and features twenty leading thinkers and doers arguing for or against provocative resolutions that address pressing public policy concerns such as the future of global security, the implications of humanitarian intervention, the effectiveness of foreign aid, the threat of climate change, and the state of health care in Canada and the United States.

"By trying to highlight the most important issues at crucial moments in the global conversation, these debates not only profile the ideas and solutions of some of our brightest thinkers and doers, but crystallize public passion and knowledge, helping to tackle some global challenges confronting humankind." — Peter Munk

houseofanansi.com/collections/munk-debates

CPSIA information can be obtained
at www.ICGtesting.com
Printed in the USA
LVOW03s0510080218
565737LV00001B/1/P